LOOKING AT LANDSCAPES

Flooding and Drought

Clive Gifford

Evans

First published in paperback in 2009 by Evans Brothers Limited
2A Portman Mansions
Chiltern Street
London W1U 6NR

British Library Cataloguing in Publication Data
Gifford, Clive
Flooding and Drought. - (Looking at landscapes)
1. Floods - Juvenile literature
2. Droughts - Juvenile literature
I. Title
551.5'773

ISBN 9780237540296

Consultant: Simon Ross
Editor: Sonya Newland
Designer: Big Blu Ltd
Picture researcher: Julia Bird

LOOKING AT LANDSCAPES
Flooding and Drought

Contents

Introduction   6

Water on the Move   8

Floods: Causes and Impacts   16

Droughts: Causes and Impacts   26

Living with Floods and Droughts   34

Glossary   42

Further Information   44

Index   45

Introduction

Water is essential to life on Earth; all living things need it in order to survive and flourish. Water is the major constituent of living matter – between 50 and 90 per cent of the weight of all living organisms, from microscopic bacteria to giant blue whales, is water. On our planet, water exists in all three states of matter: as a solid in the form of ice, as a liquid in the forms of freshwater and seawater, and as a gas in the form of water vapour.

There is a vast amount of water on the planet, but its distribution is varied. Many regions have plenty of water, while others have very little. Too much water, or too little, are two of the world's most serious natural hazards.

A flood occurs when a body of water rises and overflows on to normally dry land. Floods can

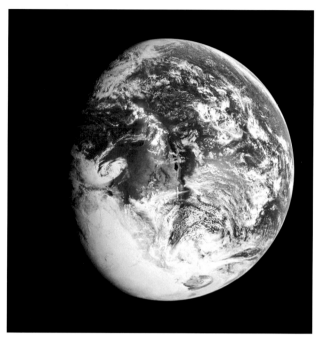

▲ From space, our planet is a mass of blue – the oceans make up 70 per cent of the Earth's surface.

▼ Droughts – long periods without rainfall – combined with human factors such as using water for agriculture, can cause lakes, rivers and even inland seas to dry up completely. This barren area in Australia was once a lake.

▲ In some parts of the world floods can create fertile land for farming. Here, farmers in Burma plough a rice field on a floodplain.

bring benefits to local populations, such as helping to create fertile soil that is good for farming, but they can also bring destruction and misery to human settlements. Floods can wash away crops and valuable soil, and cause landslides or mudslides that engulf villages and cause destruction to property and even loss of life. They can also damage or destroy infrastructures such as transport and communication links, making rescue attempts extremely difficult. Floods can damage sewage and other waste-disposal systems, which means that water supplies can become contaminated, greatly increasing the threat of disease.

Droughts may not be as quick, dramatic or spectacular as the raging torrents of water produced by some floods, but they are equally – if not more – devastating. Droughts are long periods in which a region experiences an abnormally low level of rainfall, or no rain at all. This is the most serious physical hazard to agriculture in nearly every part of the world. It can cause soils to dry out, plants and crops to die, and streams, lakes and rivers to dry up. At its worst, drought can result in widespread famine and death for thousands of people.

Water on the Move

Water is on the move in rivers, oceans, in the ground and high in the atmosphere. The movement of water is one of several factors that can influence climate and weather conditions which, in turn, are a major cause of floods and droughts. Climate describes the average weather conditions experienced by a particular area over a certain time; scientists usually use a period of 30 years when establishing a region's climate.

Tree transpiration

In a single hour on a very warm day, the leaves of one large oak tree can release as much as 200 litres of water as water vapour through the process of transpiration. One hectare of tropical forest can release 200,000 litres of water vapour into the atmosphere in a day.

▼ During the water cycle, heat makes water evaporate into the atmosphere. It then falls back to Earth as precipitation, where it returns to lakes, rivers and seas, or is collected back from the soil by plants. Once this has happened, the cycle begins again.

What is the water cycle?

The water on our planet is always on the move. It circulates constantly through different states and in different locations. This is known as the water cycle.

The water cycle is driven by energy from the Sun. Heat from the Sun causes water to turn from a liquid into gaseous water vapour. This gradual transformation – which occurs without the water boiling – is called evaporation. Around four-fifths of all evaporation comes from the oceans; the remaining one-fifth comes from inland water bodies such as rivers and lakes, and from vegetation. The evaporation of water into the atmosphere from the leaves and stems of plants is called transpiration. Plants absorb water from the soil through their roots and transport it through their stems and trunks to their leaves.

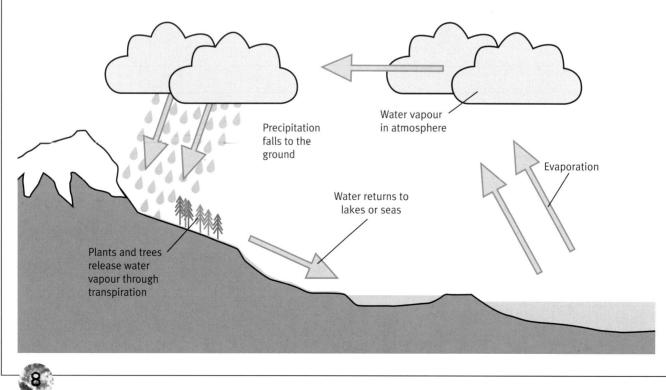

Precipitation falls to the ground

Water vapour in atmosphere

Evaporation

Water returns to lakes or seas

Plants and trees release water vapour through transpiration

Rainfall – seen here at the bottom centre – is the result of the cooling and condensation of moisture by wind.

Most water is transpired by plants through small pores or openings called stomata, found on the underside of leaves.

Winds transport the evaporated water around the globe, influencing the levels of humidity (the amount of moisture carried in the atmosphere) throughout the world. Clouds form when warm air containing water vapour rises and then cools. The vapour condenses to form millions of tiny water droplets; these collide with each other to create larger droplets. Eventually they become too heavy for the air to support, and fall back to Earth as rain.

Water that falls on to the Earth's surface from clouds is called precipitation. The type of precipitation that occurs depends largely on temperature and air pressure. Rain is the most common form, but snow, sleet and hail are also forms of precipitation. Snowflakes form when water droplets freeze into ice crystals in clouds and then fall to

▲ This microscopic image shows the tiny pores, or stomata, on the underside of leaves, magnified to around 400 times their actual size. These act rather like the pores in human skin, allowing water to pass out of the leaf in a process called transpiration.

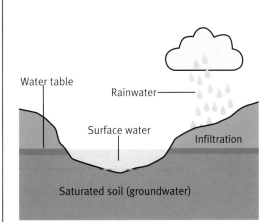

Water table
Rainwater
Surface water
Infiltration
Saturated soil (groundwater)

▲ When rainwater hits the ground, some of it will penetrate the surface (infiltration). A certain amount (groundwater) is drawn back up through the roots of trees and plants. The rest sinks to the water table.

▼ This is the 'Middle of the World' monument, situated on the equator in Ecuador. Here, and all along the equator, temperatures are high because the Sun's rays strike the Earth almost directly.

the ground through cold air. Sleet is a mixture of snow and rain. It is created when rain encounters a layer of very cold air close to the ground; in this case some, but not all, of the rain freezes.

Once the water reaches the ground, one of a number of processes may occur. Some of the water may be trapped or intercepted by plants and then transpired back into the atmosphere. Some water also forms small pools or puddles on the ground; much of this evaporates back into the atmosphere. Water may penetrate the surface of the land in a process called infiltration. Infiltration can occur at different rates depending on the composition of the soil. For example, a sandy soil with lots of air spaces between the sand grains allows rapid infiltration, whereas in a clay soil, with much smaller spaces between the particles, infiltration is much slower. A portion of this water, called groundwater, will be drawn up by the roots of plants and released back into the atmosphere via transpiration. Some groundwater sinks until it reaches the water table – the top surface of the saturation zone, where all the air spaces in the soil and rock have become filled with water. Much groundwater travels sideways along locations known as aquifers, and eventually seeps into oceans, rivers and streams. The rest of the water that remains on the Earth's surface is called runoff. Runoff eventually empties into streams, rivers and lakes, which gradually carry it back towards the oceans.

What factors influence climate?

Climates vary around the world and many factors influence them. Among these are the region's latitude (its distance from the equator), the circulation of air currents and winds, and the movement of water in the world's oceans.

How the Sun's rays strike the Earth's surface can determine the temperature of a region, which affects its climate and weather patterns. Because the surface of the Earth is curved, different parts of the planet receive different amounts of the Sun's rays. Around the centre of the Earth – the equator – temperatures remain high and do not vary much, because the Sun's rays strike this region almost directly all year round and the Sun's energy is more

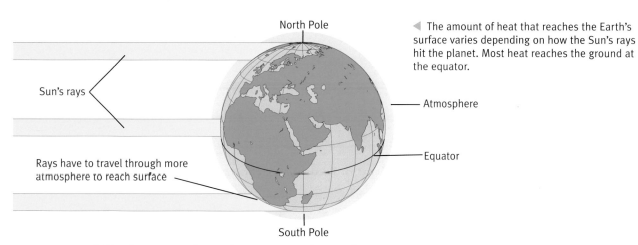

North Pole

Sun's rays

Rays have to travel through more
atmosphere to reach surface

South Pole

◀ The amount of heat that reaches the Earth's
surface varies depending on how the Sun's rays
hit the planet. Most heat reaches the ground at
the equator.

Atmosphere

Equator

concentrated. Further away from the equator, the angle
with which the Sun's rays strike the surface is greater. This
means that they have to travel through more of the Earth's
heat-absorbing atmosphere, and that their energy is spread
over a wider surface area, which reduces the warming effect
of the rays. This is rather like a torch beam that appears
elongated and dim when the torch is held at an oblique
angle to a surface. The polar regions – the furthest points
away from the equator – are the coldest on Earth.

▼ Earth is coldest at the poles, in areas like the
Antarctic, because the Sun's rays have to pass
through more atmosphere in the polar regions,
and this absorbs more heat.

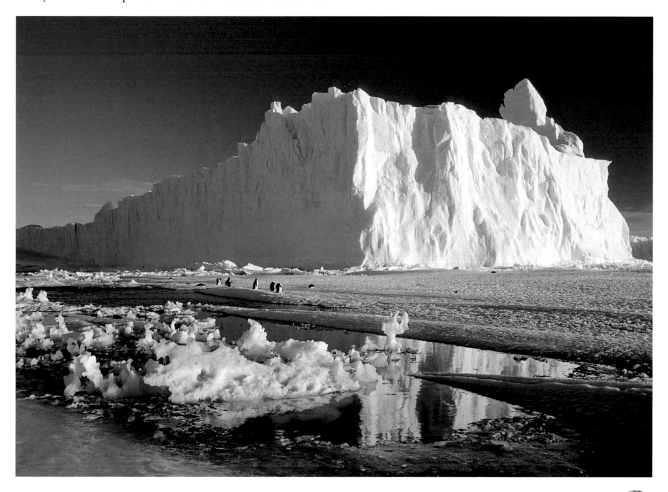

What are high and low air pressure?

Air pressure is the weight or mass of the atmosphere pushing down on the Earth's surface. As air in the Earth's atmosphere is always on the move, so air pressure constantly varies from place to place. At the surface, air moves from areas of high pressure (called anticyclones) to areas of low pressure (called cyclones or depressions). This movement of air is wind.

Scientists have identified a number of circulation cells in the atmosphere, where air moves across the latitudes. As air rises and falls within these cells it affects the air pressure at the ground surface. In areas where air rises (for example, at the equator) low-pressure areas are formed. Where air sinks (for example at about 30 degrees north and south), areas of high pressure are formed.

Areas of high pressure tend to bring hot, dry weather in summer and cold, dry weather in winter. This is because air is usually sinking and is therefore unlikely to form clouds and rain. Low-pressure areas, with their associated rising air, tend to bring clouds, rain or snow. Over seas and oceans, intense low-pressure areas can result in storm surges that may lead to rises in sea level; this is a major cause of coastal flooding (see page 22).

How do ocean currents affect climate?

The Earth's climate is affected by the water in the oceans and its ability to absorb large quantities of the Sun's heat. Amazingly, the top two metres of an ocean store more heat than the whole of the Earth's atmosphere! Ocean currents carry much of this heat around the world and towards the polar regions. In this way, heat is redistributed and the global heat balance is maintained. This heat warms land masses as well as the lower atmosphere above the ocean. One major ocean current, the Gulf Stream, carries warmth towards northern Europe, giving the region a mild climate. Oceans tend to moderate the climate of coastal regions, reducing the extremes of temperature found there. Areas far inland usually have more extreme temperature differences between their winters and summers, and they are usually drier.

▲ This is a low-pressure weather system over Australia. The swirling clouds bring stormy but humid weather. Sometimes they become so intense that they form a hurricane or typhoon.

🌐 North Sea storm surge

Storm surges are abnormal rises in sea levels. They occur most frequently in areas of the world that are prone to massive storms including hurricanes, such as Asia and the Gulf of Mexico. However, these are not the only places that can suffer. In January 1953, a giant storm surge in the southern North Sea resulted in a sea-level rise of over 3 metres. Catastrophic flooding occurred on the coasts of England and the Netherlands, claiming over 2,200 lives.

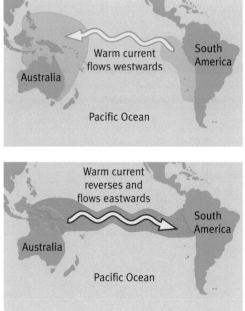

Ocean currents affect the climates of different regions. When major currents change, it can have a huge impact on climate. In the Pacific Ocean, the reversal of currents is called El Niño. During this time, the warm current flows eastwards, resulting in floods in America and reduced rainfall in South-East Asia and Australia.

Occasionally, major ocean currents alter their direction, and this can have a significant effect on the climate. In the Pacific, surface ocean currents normally transport warmer water westwards towards Australia. El Niño is the name given to a complex series of changes in weather conditions caused by the reversal in the currents of the Pacific Ocean. During El Niño, the warm current flows eastwards, creating more water vapour in the air over parts of South America, Central America and the United States. This leads to heavier rainfalls and floods in these regions, while drought conditions occur in the west Pacific, including Australia and Indonesia. Climate can be affected all over the world

🌐 Water proportions

Seas and oceans contain 97.5 per cent of the Earth's water; the land holds 2.4 per cent; and the atmosphere contains less than one-thousandth of a per cent.

▲ Deforestation is believed to be a major cause of the greenhouse effect. As trees are cut down, more greenhouse gases can be trapped in the atmosphere, warming the planet.

▶ In 2008, Australia was still experiencing its worst drought since reliable records began in 1910. Australian scientists believe that global warming was a major cause of the drought. It was concentrated in eastern Australia, in the Murray-Darling Basin – the nation's agricultural heartland, which produces two-fifths of all Australia's agricultural output.

by the El Niño phenomenon. The giant El Niño of 1997–98 disrupted weather patterns around the globe, resulting in droughts, floods and storms that killed an estimated 2,100 people.

How is global warming related to floods and droughts?

Temperature records indicate that the planet is getting warmer; scientists have called this trend 'global warming'. In the past 100 years, there have also been more reported instances of droughts and floods than ever before. Many scientists believe that the two phenomena are linked and that part of the change in global climate is due to the greenhouse effect.

Global warming is a complex process and no one is certain what will occur in the future. Some scientists think that global warming could enhance the speed at which the water cycle occurs. Rates of evaporation could increase, resulting in widespread drought conditions as well as potentially making weather more unpredictable. Warmer and wetter conditions caused by global warming may increase flooding in some areas, while an increase in global temperatures will cause sea levels to rise (water expands as it warms up). The Intergovernmental Panel on Climate Change reports that sea levels could rise by over 60 cm by the twenty-second century. This would result in huge areas of land being submerged – the US Environmental Protection Agency estimates that as much as 57,000 km² of America's eastern coastline could be under threat. This is just a tiny fraction of all the land that could be submerged around the world, which would particularly affect the millions of people living in low-lying delta regions such as Bangladesh.

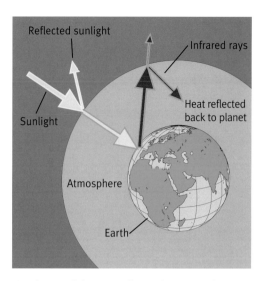

▲ When sunlight enters the Earth's atmosphere and strikes the planet's surface, some of the Sun's energy is reflected back as heat in the form of infrared radiation. Greenhouse gases absorb this radiation, trapping heat in the atmosphere and warming the planet.

🌏 Greenhouse gases

Greenhouse gases, such as carbon dioxide, methane and nitrous oxide, are naturally present in the Earth's atmosphere and perform a vital role, helping to trap some of the Sun's energy as heat, effectively warming the surface of the planet. Because of an increase in the concentrations of greenhouse gases in the atmosphere, more heat is being trapped. This has risen by as much as 25 per cent in the past 150 years. Deforestation (the removal of trees and plant cover from the land) and the burning of large quantities of fossil fuels in industry and by motor vehicles, are major causes of this increase. Scientists are concerned about the rate of increase, and the way it might affect our planet in the future.

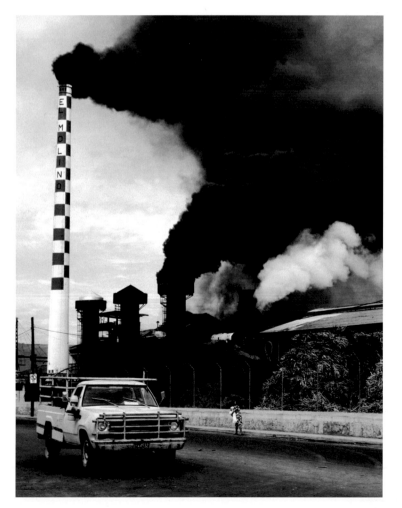

▶ Air pollution from the burning of fossil fuels in industry and by motor vehicles is one of the major causes of the greenhouse effect.

Floods: Causes and Impacts

After fire, floods are the most common and widespread of all natural disasters. In the United States alone, property damage from flooding totals over $5 billion per year.

Rivers change as they progress from young, fast-moving bodies of water in steeper areas to slow-moving, mature rivers, which often meander in large curves across flat lands before reaching the sea. Material eroded by rivers in the uplands builds up as sediment, which is then carried by the river in its lower course. Large rivers transport enormous amounts of sediment – the Mississippi River, for example, empties approximately 300 million cubic metres of sediment into the Gulf of Mexico every year. This sediment is finally deposited in one of two ways. It can be left at the mouth of the river where it empties

▼ In China, huge areas of a floodplain are often terraced and used to cultivate crops like rice, which grows well in the saturated soil. This is just one example of how flooding can have positive effects.

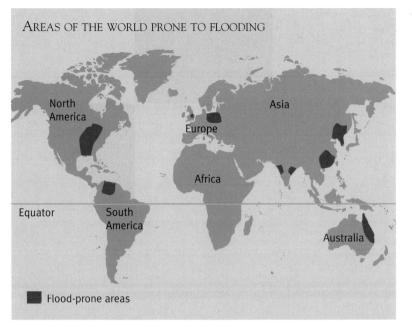

AREAS OF THE WORLD PRONE TO FLOODING

North America

Europe

Asia

Africa

Equator

South America

Australia

■ Flood-prone areas

◀ This map shows the parts of the world that are particularly prone to flooding disasters. Such floods are usually caused by sudden, heavy or prolonged rainfall.

into the sea; over time, layers of sediment can build up to form an area of flat land called a delta. Sediment can also be deposited by the river bursting its banks or flooding along its course. During a river flood, the sediment is deposited on the land either side of the river.

Over many years of repeated floods, layers of extremely fertile land build up; these are known as floodplains or alluvial plains. Floodplains have been vital to the development of human life. Many early civilisations grew up around them, close to rivers such as the Nile in Egypt, the Indus and the Ganges in India, and China's Huang He. Today, these and other floodplains are inhabited by millions of people who rely on the fertile land for food, even though the risk of flooding remains a constant concern.

What are cyclical floods?

Many floods are cyclical, which means they occur regularly, often caused by a cycle of rains, or snow and ice melting. For example, the monsoons that occur in Asia bring regular and welcome rains that are essential to crop-growing in the region. However, they can also cause flooding of river deltas and floodplains. The River Nile runs through Egypt, and for thousands of years its annual flooding not only brought vital waters but also rich, fertile sediments to the fields either side of the river. The Egyptians referred to the annual flooding as the 'Gift of the Nile' (see page 38).

▲ This satellite image shows the Nile delta. The fertile region, where the river Nile floods its banks, can be seen in red at the top left of the picture. Settlements grew up around areas like this because the land was fertile and good for farming. The Egyptian capital Cairo is the tiny grey area right at the base of the delta.

Measuring floods

One way of measuring the magnitude, or scale, of a flood is to compare it to how often such a size flood is expected to occur. Floods can be 10-, 100-, 500- or 1,000-year occurrences. For example, a 10-year flood is a level of river discharge that has a probability of occurring once every 10 years on average. Such an event is a lot smaller than a 100-year flood, which is only likely to occur on average once every 100 years. Remember, however, that these probabilities are long-term and there is no reason why two large floods couldn't happen in consecutive years. The Big Thompson river valley flood (see page 20) was a once every 1,000-year flood.

▼ There are several reasons why regions around rivers can flood. These include heavy rains, melting ice and snow, storm surges, human land use, and the failure of dams.

What are the main causes of river floods?

River floods can be caused by a number of different factors. The most common of these is a torrential storm or a long period of heavy rain. Flooding occurs when there is too much water for a river channel to contain, and the excess water simply spills over the top of the banks. During a storm there is often a huge amount of water falling on a drainage basin in a very short period of time, and the river channels cannot cope with the volume of water surging down the streams and tributaries.

The rate at which soil absorbs water decreases with continuous wetting. The longer a rainstorm lasts, the more likely it is that rainwater will flow across the ground as surface runoff and enter streams and rivers. The amount of water that can be held in the soil depends upon its porosity – the proportion of pore spaces in the soil. The ability of water to flow through the soil depends upon its permeability; if there are lots of pores or underground channels then water will pass through the soil freely. Under such conditions the soil is said to be permeable; if water does not pass through the soil, it is said to be impermeable. When the entire area below the ground is saturated, further water is forced to remain on the surface.

Different land surfaces hold different amounts of water and absorb it at different rates. Flooding is common in winter and early spring when the ground can be frozen and impermeable. This means that most rainwater and meltwater from snow and ice become surface runoff.

Dams can fail and suddenly release large amounts of water

Areas with steep slopes suffer flash floods

Heavy rains and monsoons saturate the soil

Flooding of coastal areas is caused by storm surges and tsunamis

Snow and ice melt rapidly in spring when the temperature rises sharply

Deforestation results in soil erosion, leading to surface runoff and subsequent flooding

Human activity such as agriculture prevents floodplains from soaking up water

🌐 China's river floods

In the last 2,000 years, the Yangtze River in China has flooded more than 1,000 times. However, it is another river, the Huang He, that has been responsible for China's most disastrous floods. The river has a very high silt content and this chokes the channel, causing the river to overflow. In 1887 flooding killed nearly two million people; in 1931 the death toll was almost four million; and in 1938 it was almost one million.

▶ In China, a boy sits of the roof of his house – the only place to escape the flood waters.

How can snowmelt and ice jams cause flooding?

Rapidly melting snow or thawing ice can create enormous amounts of water. This can upset the balance of the water cycle in a region and may result in flooding. An ice jam can occur when parts of a frozen river thaw and melt at different rates to other parts. High levels of water become trapped behind still-frozen river ice and can flood the surrounding area. In February 2003, an ice jam on the Exploits River in Canada caused a major flood that swept through the town of Badger in Newfoundland; 1,200 people were evacuated from their homes.

▼ This is a melting polar ice cap. When large bodies of frozen water like this begin to melt they can sweep through a region and overflow river banks, creating massive floods.

What are flash floods?

Flash floods are floods that occur quickly, usually within six hours of the start of heavy rainfall. Cloudburst floods are a type of flash flood caused by very intense rainfall, usually more than 250 mm per hour. A relatively small number of flash floods are caused by sudden snowmelt or ice jams.

Flash floods, like this one in Montana, USA, are caused by sudden heavy downpours of rain.

Flash floods are more common in mountainous areas, where steep slopes cause water to travel at high speeds. Although flash floods tend to occur quickly and last only a short time, they can still be devastating because they usually come with little warning. If a man-made dam holding back huge quantities of water fails, it can also cause destructive flash floods.

Can human activity cause floods?

Human impact on land areas can create conditions in which floods are more likely. For example, the removal of tree cover through deforestation (see page 33) deprives land of the vegetation that intercepts and soaks up large amounts of rainfall. Without trees, more water than the land can absorb through infiltration may reach the ground during heavy rains. The excess water becomes surface runoff, carrying loose soil that is no longer bound together by tree and plant roots. This soil can clog rivers and lakes with sediment, making floods more likely.

The Big Thompson flash flood

The Big Thompson river valley was a popular destination for campers and walkers in the American state of Colorado. In July 1976, a thunderstorm resulted in 30 cm of rainfall in four and a half hours. Two thirds of that rain fell in less than an hour. A severe flash flood raged down the river valley, sweeping 3-metre-wide boulders in front of it. Houses, vehicles and camper vans had no chance of escape. During that short time over 140 people were killed, 418 houses were destroyed and more than $40 million of damage was wrought.

Some floods are a result of deliberate or accidental human action. Occasionally these are caused by the construction of dams to form a reservoir intended to supply settlements or industry with water, or to concentrate the natural fall of a river at one location to maximise the amount of energy that can be used by a hydroelectric power plant. Poor dam and reservoir construction can cause floods that lead to widespread destruction. In 1963, in north-eastern Italy, a giant landslide fell into a water reservoir held in place by the Vaiont Dam. The landslide generated a wave that powered over the top of the dam and destroyed a number of nearby settlements, killing more than 2,500 people. Amazingly the dam remained intact! The area had been prone to landslides in the past and was a high-risk site for building a large dam and reservoir.

Urbanisation – the growing in size of towns and cities – has resulted in much previously undeveloped land being covered in stone, concrete and other impermeable materials to form car parks, roads and pavements. Unless drainage systems are carefully planned and constructed, rainwater cannot be absorbed into the ground fast enough and becomes surface runoff. Heavy and prolonged rainfall can easily cause an urban flood, which fills these car parks and overflows to submerge nearby roads and flood buildings below ground level.

▲ Flooding can cause serious damage to property in built-up areas, where concrete roads prevent water from being easily absorbed. This flood warning sign is in a residential area in the UK.

🌐 The Buffalo Creek disaster

A dam at Buffalo Creek in the American state of West Virginia was used to store waste material from coal-mining, and this included a large amount of water. In February 1972, after three days of heavy rains, the dam collapsed, sending tonnes of water down the valley. The resulting flood killed 118 people in settlements nearby and caused nearly $70 million of damage.

▶ A row of houses in the coal-mining town of Buffalo Creek, West Virginia, is destroyed when the dam collapses, sending a cascade of water downstream.

What causes coastal flooding?

Seas and oceans cover almost three-quarters of the Earth's surface, and nearly half of the world's population lives within 60 km of a coastline. When the sea level rises and overflows into coastal regions, therefore, the floods can cause widespread destruction and loss of life. Such rises in sea level and coastal flooding are caused by several phenomena, including global warming (see page 14), tsunamis (see page 24) and hurricanes (see page 23).

Ocean storms can transport large quantities of water to coastal regions. Such storms are usually caused by an intense area of low pressure, which can raise the sea level in that region. These storm-related rises in sea level are called storm surges, and they can result in coastal flooding in many parts of the world.

▲ The city of Venice in Italy has been subject to coastal flooding caused by rises in sea level and the fact that the city itself is gradually sinking. In 2003, construction began on a sea gate, which – it is hoped – will protect this ancient city and its beautiful historic buildings from the threat of further floods. In December 2008 flooding in Venice rose to its highest level in more than 20 years.

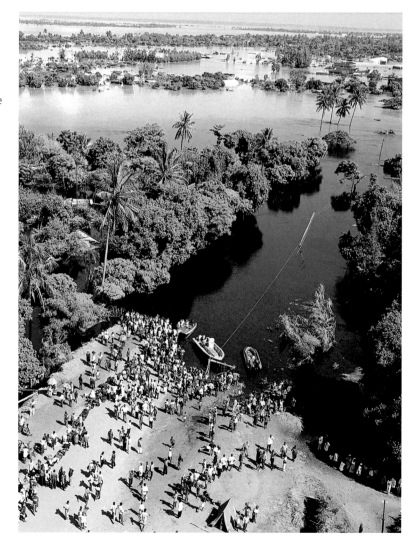

▶ Hundreds of people flee their homes as floods hit Chibuto in Mozambique. These floods were caused by unexpected levels of rainfall, which made the sea level rise and move inland.

🌍 Sea-level rise in Bangladesh

A storm at the mouth of the River Ganges in Bangladesh in August 2004 caused a flood that eventually covered almost two-thirds of the country. The disaster affected nearly 30 million people, many of whom found that their homes were destroyed and that they were cut off from food and other supplies. The problems in Bangladesh continued for months, as diseases carried in the water infected the population.

▼ Parts of Bangladesh have suffered from periodic flooding in the delta region. Here, people are forced to travel by boat on the flood water that swept the country in August 2004.

🌍 Hurricanes

Hurricanes, also known as tropical cyclones or typhoons, are fierce, spiralling storms that form over the oceans of the tropics. Hurricanes have an intense low-pressure core, sucking in warm moist air that rises rapidly to form towering thunderstorm clouds. Hurricanes are associated with high wind speeds, averaging 120 kph, and with gusts in excess of 200 kph. Torrential rainfall occurs, often leading to flooding as rivers burst their banks.

◄ The high winds of Hurricane Frances cause flooding in a car park in Florida, USA, in September 2004.

Can tides cause floods?

Tides are the regular rise and fall of the sea level caused by the gravitational pull of the Sun and the Moon on the Earth's oceans. Tides move inland and back twice every 24 hours. In the open sea, the movement of the water is hardly noticeable. However, in some coastal areas – such as those with narrow bays – the tidal difference is significant. The tidal range is the vertical height difference between high tide – when the sea level is highest – and low tide, when it is at its lowest. Tidal ranges can be as little as half a metre, but along some coastlines they can be far greater. The tidal range on the south coast of Britain near the outlet of the River Thames, is approximately 6 metres. In the Bay of Fundy, in south-eastern Canada, the tidal range is over 16 metres. Regular high tides are predictable, and rarely produce flooding on their own. However, when a very high tide coincides with a moderate or severe storm, flooding can occur.

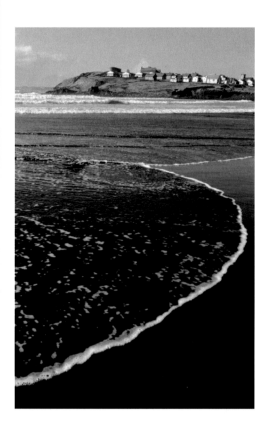

▶ During high tide, sea waters move up the beaches, drawing closer to settlements; at low tide, they recede far back. This picture shows high tide near a village in the Pribilof Islands in Alaska.

▶ Every 14 days, the Moon and the Sun are aligned and both exert a gravitational pull on the Earth's seas and oceans. As a result, higher than-usual tides, called spring tides, occur, which can cause flooding.

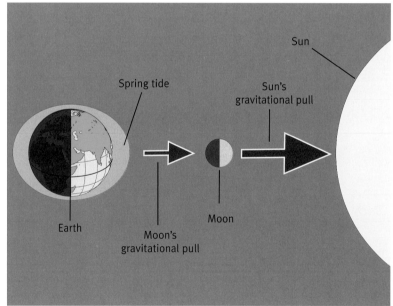

Spring tide
Sun
Sun's gravitational pull
Earth
Moon
Moon's gravitational pull

What are tsunamis?

Tsunamis are destructive waves that sweep in from the ocean. They are sometimes known as tidal waves, although this is misleading as they are not caused by or related to tidal movement. They are usually the result of a volcanic eruption, a giant landslide, or an earthquake that occurs under the sea.

🌀 The Asian tsunami

On 26 December 2004, an earthquake measuring 9.1 on the Richter scale occurred in the Indian Ocean near Sumatra. It caused a series of tsunamis that devastated 11 countries across Asia. The effects were felt as far away as Africa, nearly 5,000 km from the epicentre. As no warning system exists in the Indian Ocean, the damage was severe. UN figures state that 229,866 people were lost, including 186,983 people dead and 42,883 missing. It prompted a massive humanitarian response.

A tsunami can travel tens or even hundreds of kilometres across the ocean, reaching speeds of up to 800 kph. As a tsunami leaves the deep water of the open ocean and travels into the shallower water near the coast, it transforms. Its speed decreases, although it still travels rapidly and with great force, but as it slows down, its height increases. Out at sea, a tsunami may appear as a wave only half to one metre high and be hardly noticeable. However, by the time it reaches the coast, it might have grown to a wall of water more than 15 metres high.

Tsunamis lose energy as they hit the shoreline but they still arrive with vast amounts of energy, capable of destroying entire coastal settlements and travelling inland several kilometres. Tsunamis can have great powers of erosion, stripping land of its vegetation and beaches of their sand.

The most recent major tsunami occurred in December 2004. Caused by an undersea earthquake off the Indonesian coast, the tsunamis surged across the Indian Ocean at great speeds. The province of Aceh in northern Indonesia was the closest inhabited area to the earthquake's epicentre and was the first hit. Within the next few hours, the tsunamis devastated coastlines all across Asia, with waves reaching heights of 15 metres as they swept inland. Buildings were destroyed in an instant and whole communities were wiped out.

▲ A massive wave strikes Penang in Malaysia in December 2004. There was little warning that the tsunamis were about to hit, and many people did not understand the danger they were in. People were killed or injured as the waves crashed over buildings, or they were sucked out to sea as the water receded.

▼ Men in Nicaragua try to salvage parts of their home after it was destroyed by a tsunami in 1992.

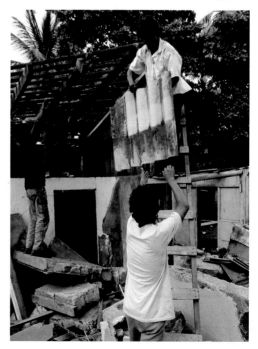

Droughts: Causes and Impacts

Many parts of the world experience a dry climate with a lack of rainfall. Desert regions – areas that receive less than 250 mm of rainfall per year – cover more than a tenth of the land on Earth. Many species of animals and plants have learned to adapt to the harsh desert climates and environments. However, during a drought much harsher conditions prevail, and many people may die or be forced to move away from their homes.

▲ A drought is defined as a period in which an area experiences lower levels of rainfall than normal, causing the ground to dry out. Here, a farmer stands beside what remains of a lake in North Dakota, USA, during a period of drought in the 1990s.

Drought can best be defined as an extended period in which rainfall levels are below those normally expected in a particular region. This can lead to a long-term depletion of groundwater and the stunting or dying of plants due to lack of water. Although we tend to associate droughts with the desert areas of the world, they can occur almost anywhere. In the UK, for example, where rainfall is usually quite high, a drought struck in 1976; reservoirs dried up and people had to collect freshwater from standpipes in the street, or from water tankers.

Droughts can be classified regionally according to the amount of rainfall that the region normally receives. For example, in the United States, a drought is defined as 21 days with only 30 per cent of the average rain for that area. In India, a drought occurs when monsoon rains are much weaker than usual. When rainfall is more than 30 per cent

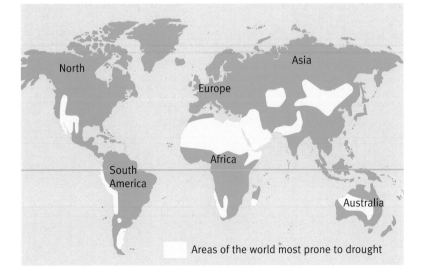

▶ This map shows the parts of the world that are most prone to drought, including the vast areas of desert in places like North Africa and central Australia.

Areas of the world most prone to drought

lower than normal and more than 20 per cent of an area of the country is under drought, the situation is called an all-India drought. The beginning of a drought is especially difficult to determine. Weeks or many months may elapse before it is clear that a drought is occurring. A period of lower-than-average rainfall may not always signal the start of a drought, as dry spells occur throughout the world.

▲ The Atacama Desert in northern Chile is one of the driest regions on Earth. In 1971, rain fell for the first time in around 400 years.

Where do droughts occur?

During the mid-1980s, people in wealthier, more developed countries such as the United States and many European nations were shocked by television and newspaper images from Ethiopia. These showed massive suffering and death from famine (a severe shortage of food), disease and lack of water. This was caused in part by a civil war in the country, which meant that food distribution was not efficient, but the key factor in the famine was a fierce drought that had struck the country. As a result of this high-profile example, many people associate droughts with parts of Africa, particularly the fringes of the world's largest desert, the Sahara. The reality is that they are far more

🌐 Measuring drought

The Palmer Drought Severity Index is one of several measuring systems for droughts. It uses temperature and rainfall data to indicate which areas of a country are more likely to be affected by drought. The index uses 0 as normal, and drought is shown in terms of negative numbers; for example, -2 is a moderate drought, -3 is a severe drought, and -4 is an extreme drought.

▶ In many drought-ridden regions, facilities like this water pump in Kabul can save lives, although many people have to travel long distances to collect the water for drinking and washing.

common and widespread than this. For example, in 2002 severe droughts again struck Ethiopia, but also parts of the United States, Australia, central America and Asia.

Despite this, droughts do occur most frequently in regions on the edges of hot deserts, usually the driest parts of the planet. Rain falling from clouds above these areas often has to pass through thousands of metres of air. Because of the heat and the distance it falls, much of the rain evaporates before it reaches the ground.

▼ The Sahara is the largest desert in the world. Around its edges, where people live, droughts are common because much of the rain in the atmosphere evaporates before it reaches the ground.

During the water cycle, water is released as vapour back into the atmosphere by means of evaporation and through transpiration from plants. The total amount

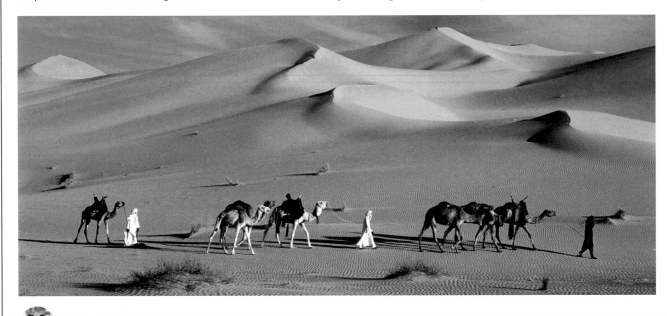

of water returned to the atmosphere by these processes is called evapotranspiration. The rate of evapotranspiration can vary greatly depending on the temperature, humidity and winds in an area. When evapotranspiration rates are high – increased by sunlight and long periods of heat – soil loses moisture rapidly and extremely dry conditions develop. As plants die, the food supplies for people and animals disappear.

Drought in North America

North America experienced a three-year drought between 1987 and 1989. The drought began along the west coast of the USA and spread into north-western regions and southern Canada. At its peak, an estimated 36 per cent of the United States was in drought. Wildfires raged through the world-famous Yellowstone Park in 1988, but the greatest damage was to agriculture. The total cost of the drought was estimated at over $36 billion.

◀ These maize plants have withered and died due to lack of rainfall in Texas, in the USA. At its worst, the drought in North America covered more than a third of the country.

What causes droughts?

Droughts involve a complex series of processes that are still being researched. Climate change brought on by global warming may be increasing the risk of droughts in some regions. Variations in climate and weather caused by changes in winds and ocean currents such as El Niño (see page 13) are believed to be the cause of many droughts across the world.

Another weather condition that can give rise to droughts is an area of high air pressure called a blocking high. A blocking high usually remains stationary for a long period of time and effectively forces any areas of low pressure, which carries clouds and rain, around it. An area of land that lies underneath a particularly strong and long-term blocking high may experience a drought. This

▲ Droughts are often caused by a lack of precipitation, but they can also be a result of hot dry winds, which remove moisture from the soil so nothing can grow.

▼ This diagram shows the way air rises and falls over mountains, creating rain-shadow areas. Most of the rain falls in the mountains; any precipitation that is left is picked up by the warm dry air, leaving a desert area.

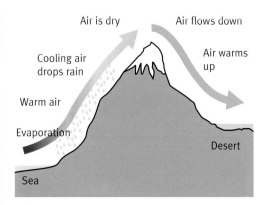

Air is dry

Air flows down

Cooling air
drops rain

Air warms
up

Warm air

Evaporation

Desert

Sea

phenomenon is believed to be responsible for most of the droughts that affect the American state of California, for example. A blocking high created the drought conditions in Britain and much of western Europe in 1976 (see page 26).

Some areas of the world are prone to droughts because of their geographical location. A rain-shadow area, for example, can occur when a range of mountains lies in the path of rain-carrying winds from the sea. The air is forced to cool down as it rises over the mountains and it releases almost all the water it is carrying as rain. When the air starts to sink on the leeward (sheltered) side of the mountains it becomes warmer and drier. This is called the rain-shadow effect, and it explains why areas on the leeward side of mountains are much drier than those on the windward (exposed) side. A rain-shadow area may become a desert or may experience droughts. The Great Dividing Range in Australia and the Rocky Mountains of North America both create rain-shadow areas that suffer from periodic drought conditions.

Clouds containing water vapour can be carried long distances. However, the further they travel inland and away from the oceans, the more likely they are to have released some or most of their moisture as precipitation. In regions lying thousands of kilometres from the coast there may be very little rainfall. These places are sometimes referred to as 'continental drought regions'. The Gobi Desert in Mongolia falls into this category.

Famine

A famine is a long period of time in which an area suffers from a lack of food. Many factors can contribute to famine, including war, the general poverty in a region, earthquakes and other natural disasters. However, drought is often a major cause of famine. Almost 70 per cent of all water used by humans is diverted for agriculture. Without adequate water supplies, crops fail, livestock dies and food supplies are drastically reduced. This is why famines frequently follow prolonged droughts.

◀ In 2001 the extreme heat in and around desert regions in Australia caused bush fires, which spread dangerously close to urban areas. Some scientists attribute the increase in the number of this type of fire to global warming.

🌍 Drought in eastern Africa

In 1984, a severe drought hit eastern Africa, particularly the nations of Ethiopia, Sudan and Somalia. In northern Ethiopia, for example, there was an almost total failure of crops, as plants did not receive the levels of water they required for growth. Hundreds of thousands of people were forced to leave their homelands, and over six million became reliant on refugee camps and food aid from feeding centres supplied by countries like the UK and USA. The death toll in the region had risen to almost one million by the end of the drought.

◀ Workers carry sacks of wheat to famine-stricken villages in Ethiopia during the drought.

What happens after a drought?

Many regions of the world mostly or fully recover after a drought. Drought-stricken areas in wealthier countries receive aid with which they can replenish lands, as well as building water systems that may make a future drought less damaging. In poorer nations, the prospects can be bleak. What funding there might be is often spent on disaster relief – providing some form of food, shelter and medical attention to keep people alive – without any longer-term planning. Furthermore, money is often spent on large glamorous schemes that benefit wealthy city dwellers without helping the majority of the rural poor.

Heavy rainfall may signify the end of a drought, but it is rarely the end of the problems. Rains hit sun-baked ground and the water is often unable to infiltrate the soil. It remains on the surface, and can lead to soil erosion and powerful floods, causing more devastation. In 2003, after lengthy droughts in Kenya and Ethiopia, both regions were subject to heavy rains, resulting in floods. Around 60,000 people in Kenya and 95,000 in Ethiopia were rendered homeless.

▲ A man and a child sit on the earth in Thailand; it has been baked by the Sun and cracked due to lack of rain, so that it can no longer support life.

What is desertification?

Desertification is the expansion of desert-like conditions into areas that had previously been able to support life. While desertification can be a natural consequence of climate change, it is often brought about inadvertently by human activities, including the overgrazing of livestock, deforestation (the removal of trees and plant cover), and surface land mining.

Along with drought, these activities may result in large areas losing vegetation cover. The roots of trees and other plants bind soil together, enabling water to be absorbed and further plant life to grow. As land is cleared of its vegetation, the topsoil becomes exposed to the elements and can be washed or blown away, clogging rivers and other bodies of water with sediment. When topsoil is removed, water cannot be retained in the remaining soil and fertile land becomes arid and desert-like.

▲ In Morocco, villagers have built barriers to try to prevent desertification. The United Nations estimates that desertification claims as much as 60,000 km² of land – a quarter of the size of the United Kingdom – every year.

▲ In a 2003 study, scientists in Australia and Canada stated that pollution from western countries may have caused the droughts that ravaged Africa's Sahel region in the 1970s and 1980s. Research suggests that sulphur dioxide from factories in Europe and the USA has cooled parts of the Northern Hemisphere, driving the tropical rain belt southwards away from the Sahel.

🌍 Drought and desertification in the Sahel

The Sahel is a broad band of dry land that stretches across Africa south of the Sahara Desert. Rainfall is low, usually under 500 mm a year, and records show that it has declined by between 20 and 50 per cent since the early twentieth century. The rainfall is also unpredictable, with variations between years of 50 per cent or more. Evaporation rates are extremely high and severe droughts, which claimed the lives of thousands of people, occurred in 1972, 1975, 1984 and 1985. These devastating dry periods, as well as a significant increase in the number of people and grazing animals in the area, have seen desertification take hold of areas of the Sahel. In effect, the Sahara Desert is advancing southwards in some places at a rate of around 5 km every year.

Living with Floods and Droughts

Millions of people live in regions affected by droughts and floods. In fact, humans have shown a remarkable ability to adapt to life in these areas. For centuries nomadic peoples in desert and drought-threatened locations have migrated over large areas, developing techniques that have enabled them to survive even in the harshest conditions. In parts of South-East Asia prone to regular flooding, houses are built on stilts, keeping them away from typical high-water levels.

▼ Reforestation schemes, like this one in Costa Rica, are being carried out in many regions to reverse the effects of deforestation.

How can the impact of drought be reduced?

Lower-than-average or non-existent rainfall can strike many regions, but measures can be taken to reduce its impact. Managing the soil and keeping it in place and in good condition is vital. Steps to prevent overgrazing and the overuse of the soil by people are required in some regions, but in poorer countries, which contain thousands of farmers, it is extremely difficult to prevent people from using the land in order to survive.

In many locations around the world, reforestation schemes are being introduced. These involve planting new trees to grow forests and increase vegetation cover in areas where deforestation has occurred. Windbreaks can also help reduce the amount of soil blown away by winds, limiting the impact of soil erosion. Mulching – the placing of organic matter such as leaves, straw and sawdust to cover the ground – is a practice that can enrich the soil, keeping it in place and reducing water loss from evaporation.

The careful selection of crops suitable for the soil and climate conditions is also crucial. Dry farming depends upon efficient storage of the limited moisture in the soil, and the choice of crops and growing methods that make the best use of this moisture is important. Drought-resistant crops, such as sorghum, can reduce transpiration. Such crops may nearly cease growing during periods where there is little moisture available, but instead of dying, as many crops would do, they start to grow again when conditions become favourable.

▲ This abandoned farmhouse in Texas, photographed in 1938, shows the effect of the Dust Bowl on American farmland – plants and crops withered and died as the topsoil was blown away. The land could no longer support farming, and people were forced to leave their homes.

🌐 Dust Bowl America

A severe drought combined with poor soil-conservation techniques can lead to extreme soil erosion, which can have devastating effects on the land. This is what happened in the Great Plains region of the USA during the 1930s. Intensive farming of cereal crops and overgrazing by cattle left the soil in such poor condition that when a lengthy drought occurred, winds blew away as much as 10 cm of the topsoil. This resulted in a 'Dust Bowl'. In May 1934, a cloud of topsoil from the Great Plains blanketed the eastern regions of the USA as far as 2,400 km away. Thousands of farming families had to leave their land. It took many years of soil-conservation measures and huge US government funding to restore the land to a level that was suitable for farming once again.

Is there enough water to go round?

There is enough freshwater globally to supply the current world population; the problem lies in its distribution. In parts of Africa, the Middle East and Asia, the lack of access to clean water is a huge problem, affecting over one billion people.

Sanitation and good sewage systems are necessary to remove waste and prevent many harmful diseases. But these systems cost money to build and use large amounts of water themselves. According to the World Health Organization (WHO), over 2.4 billion people do not have access to safe sanitation systems. As a result, as many as three million people every year die from water-related diseases such as cholera. As the world population increases, so does the demand for water, but at the same time many rivers are being polluted by industrial chemicals, by runoff containing high levels of chemicals from artificial

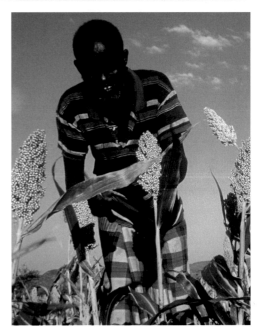

▲ Crops like sorghum – being tended here by a farmer in Ethiopia – are more resistant to arid conditions, and help the populations of drought-stricken areas to survive.

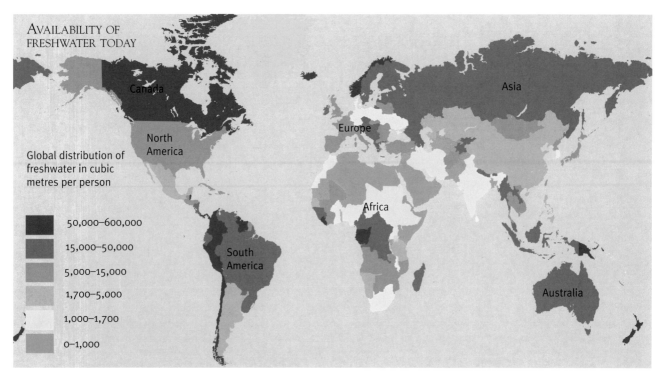

AVAILABILITY OF FRESHWATER TODAY

Canada

Asia

North America

Europe

Global distribution of freshwater in cubic metres per person

Africa

South America

Australia

■	50,000–600,000
■	15,000–50,000
■	5,000–15,000
■	1,700–5,000
□	1,000–1,700
■	0–1,000

▲ The amount of freshwater across the globe is sufficient to supply the world population. However, because it is not evenly distributed, some areas have more freshwater than the population needs, while others suffer a severe lack of it. The worst-hit areas are parts of North Africa; Canada, on the other hand, has more freshwater than it needs for the number of people who live there.

fertilisers, and from domestic sewage. This pollution is reducing the levels of fresh, clean water available in many places around the world.

Approximately one-tenth of the world's groundwater supplies are easy to reach, and much of this is being tapped by countries in order to fulfil their demands for water. Wells and bore holes are sunk deep into the ground to pump supplies of groundwater to the surface. On average, 40 per cent of the US population gets its water directly from underground sources across the country. Globally, over 1.5 billion people rely on groundwater supplies for their drinking water. However, groundwater levels can take a long time to replenish and become exhausted if used at a rapid rate.

Ancient communities in dry climates learned to conserve water and treat it as a precious commodity. The enormous rise in the world's population, and the demands on water from industry and intensive agriculture, have placed far greater strain on water resources and have increased the importance of water conservation, particularly during drought periods. Water saved by one household or village may be enough to protect the critical needs of others. Water rationing can also be employed in towns and cities to alleviate situations in an emergency.

◀ Desalination plants go some way to solving the problem of the lack of freshwater in areas like the Middle East. At plants like this one in Oman, seawater is processed to remove the salt so it can be used for agriculture and domestic purposes.

▼ Many settlements, such as this one in Cambodia, have been built around floodplains, where farmers can earn a living from the soil.

Why do so many people live in flood-threatened regions?

Floods can bring huge benefits to people. They can supply crucial water and fertile sediments to farmlands. Floods from the Himalaya mountain range, for example, deposit natural phosphates and nitrates in northern India and Bangladesh, which help to enrich the soil. Over thousands of years, sediment deposited by floods has created rich farmlands that now house a large proportion of the world's population. People have been drawn to these areas because of the flat and fertile land, which is suitable for building and provides a prosperous farming environment. Similarly, many of the world's major towns and cities are situated on or near the coast for trading purposes or fishing. Some of these settlements are in areas at risk of coastal flooding.

▶ In parts of Indonesia and China, terraces are built in the sides of hills to prevent soil erosion. Water is retained in the ground by the series of steps; this means that soil is not washed down the slope by rains.

Can flooding be controlled?

Several techniques are used to prevent floods or to control and reduce their harmful impact. Levées are embankments built on either side of a river. These can prevent smaller-scale floods from occurring, but they can force flooding to occur elsewhere on the river system. If levées break, widespread flooding can occur.

Reservoirs and dams can help control the flow of water in a region liable to flooding. In the USA, the Tennessee Valley Authority (TVA) uses a system of reservoirs and 34 dams to control flooding. Before a potential flood season, the TVA lowers the level of water stored in the reservoirs so they can hold high levels of surface runoff safely. This stored runoff is later released at a controlled rate.

In Egypt, the Aswan High Dam, which stretches across the River Nile, was completed in 1971. The dam has effectively stopped the river's annual floods by trapping its waters in a reservoir and then slowly releasing them during the dry season. However, flood control can come at a price. The farmers on the Nile have been deprived of the fertile, nutrient-rich sediment that the river's seasonal flooding used to bring. Soils in some areas are in danger of containing too much salt, which means that crops cannot grow properly, while erosion and high artificial fertiliser use creates further problems for soil quality.

🌏 Borsha and bonna floods in Bangladesh

In areas where seasonal or cyclical flooding occurs, people live a precarious existence. They rely on the flooding and channel much of its waters for farming, yet a severe flood can be disastrous. Eighty per cent of the Asian nation of Bangladesh consists of low-lying floodplains formed by two very large rivers – the Ganges and the Brahmaputra. The people of Bangladesh distinguish between regular floods called borsha and larger-than-usual floods called bonna. Bonna floods are frequently disastrous; in 1988, over 2,300 people drowned or died of disease spread by the floodwaters. Ten years later, another bonna flood covered around 66 per cent of the country, leaving more than 20 million homeless.

The Aswan Dam built across the River Nile has created a giant 480-km-long reservoir called Lake Nasser. The dam is part of a project to create large amounts of electricity from the moving waters of the river. It has also controlled annual flooding.

Flood control has also been exerted in coastal regions. Following the disastrous flooding from a coastal storm surge in 1953, the Netherlands began the Delta Plan in 1958 (it was completed in 1985). This huge project includes a series of giant dams on three river deltas, as well as the giant Stormvloedkering. This is a huge storm-surge barrier, 9 km long, capable of withstanding more than 30,000 tonnes of force from the sea. It is only lowered once a year for testing purposes or when a sea flood is imminent. At other times, it remains open, allowing sea tides to flow. In London, the Thames Barrier protects the capital from the river flooding its banks – it is the largest moveable flood barrier in the world, spanning 520 metres.

Reservoirs store water

Land management prevents overgrazing

Reforestation reduces surface runoff

Terracing reduces erosion and runoff

Water is channelled into reservoirs through irrigation schemes

Protective dykes

There are many measures that can be taken to protect both land and people from the damaging effects of flooding, including reforestation and irrigation schemes such as terracing.

▲ This storm-surge barrier, Stormvloedkering, was built in the Netherlands as part of the project to prevent damage from flooding in the delta areas. As well as this barrier, three huge dams were built between 1958 and 1985.

Is it possible to predict droughts and floods?

New technologies have made it easier to predict where and when floods may strike. Scientists create flood forecasts and issue warnings based on large amounts of data on rainfall or details of a river system and its surrounding area. This data is entered into computer systems to create a

🌐 The 1993 Mississippi flood

The Mississippi-Missouri river system drains over a quarter of the United States and has seen major flooding on a number of occasions. In 1993, torrential rainfall began in April and continued into July. The 3,000-km system of levées along the Mississippi could not hold the water and the river burst its banks, flooding more than 90,000 km² of land and causing over $10 billion of damage.

▶ An aerial view of farmland flooded by the Mississippi River in 1993.

model for the region. Warnings of major floods allow the evacuation of people from a threatened region, especially in wealthier countries with highly developed communications and transport links. Yet many local floods in wealthy countries and larger floods in poorer countries still lead to great destruction and loss of life.

Droughts are much more difficult to predict, as they are longer-term events and occur more gradually – they are not as easy to 'spot' as, for example, a hurricane. As they can strike a far larger area than floods, it is almost impossible to evacuate people from the threatened region. However, with advances in climate modelling, it may be possible to make more accurate predictions of where droughts might strike in the future. This would enable preventive action to be taken and relief and aid to reach an area more swiftly and effectively.

Future advances in weather forecasting technology and greater knowledge about the cycles and processes that shape the Earth and its climate, may lead to breakthroughs in predicting droughts or floods. In the meantime, both hazards remain a threat to ways of life all over our planet.

▼ Floods in Pennsylvania, USA, in 1972. Although recent advances in technology and improved understanding of weather patterns have resulted in better preparation for and responses to such emergencies, flooding remains a serious threat to human life and property.

Glossary

air pressure The force exerted on the Earth by the weight of the air above it. Areas of high air pressure usually have warm dry weather in summer and cold dry weather in winter. Low-pressure areas have more cloud and rain.

aquifer A sideways channel through which groundwater runs beneath the Earth.

arid Very dry.

atmosphere The layers of gases, liquids and solid particles that surround the Earth.

blocking high An area of high air pressure that remains stationary, creating low-pressure areas around it, resulting in drought conditions.

climate The long-term weather conditions in a particular region.

cloudburst flood A type of flash flood caused by sudden and intense rainfall.

condensation The change from water vapour to liquid water that occurs when air is cooled.

contaminate To poison a water supply with harmful bacteria or chemicals.

continental drought region An area far inland that experiences little or no rainfall, usually caused by the rain-shadow effect.

deflation The removal of soil from dry lands by strong winds.

deforestation The cutting down of trees and clearing away of forest areas.

delta The often triangular-shaped alluvial deposition area at the mouth of a river.

desalination The process of removing salt from seawater so it can be used for agricultural and domestic purposes.

desertification The process of expansion and spreading of a desert area, reducing the land's ability to support life.

discharge The volume of water flowing down a river, usually expressed in cubic metres per second.

drainage basin The area of land into which water from runoff, streams and tributaries feeds.

drought A period of lower-than-average rainfall that is long enough to cause hardship to people, plants and animals.

earthquake The shaking felt at the surface of the Earth caused by movement of the Earth's plates pulling apart, pushing together, or grinding alongside one another.

El Niño The name given to the weather conditions associated with the sudden reversal of ocean currents in the Pacific Ocean.

equator An imaginary line that runs round the middle of the Earth at equal distance from the North and South Poles.

erosion The movement or removal of material from a landscape.

evaporation The process by which a liquid such as water is changed into a gas when it is heated.

evapotranspiration The loss of water from the planet's surface to the atmosphere through evaporation and transpiration combined.

famine An extended period in which a country or region suffers from a severe shortage of food; famines are often a consequence of drought.

fertile Capable of growing and sustaining plant life or supporting farming.

flash flood A sudden flood that occurs shortly after or during heavy rainfall.

flood When a body of water, such as an ocean or river, rises and overflows on to the surrounding land.

floodplain A flat, low-lying area near a river or stream that is subject to flooding.

fossil fuels Materials that can be burned to generate energy; they are formed from living material that has decayed and was buried in the ground millions of years ago.

global warming The warming of the Earth's climate due to an increase in greenhouse gases trapped in the atmosphere.

greenhouse effect The rise in the Earth's temperature caused by increasing levels of greenhouse gases being trapped in the Earth's atmosphere.

greenhouse gas One of the gases present in the Earth's atmosphere – such as carbon dioxide, methane or nitrous oxide – which warm the planet.

groundwater Water stored in underground rocks.

humidity The amount of water vapour in the air.

hurricane A tropical storm that contains fast-moving, spiralling winds.

ice jam When parts of a frozen river melt at different rates, causing melted water to be blocked by the ice in front and unable to flow, leading to flooding.

impermeable Unable to absorb water easily.

infiltration The movement of water from the ground surface to the soil.

infrastructure Basic facilities and structures in countries or settlements, such as transport and communications links, and water and power supplies.

irrigation Artificial watering of the land by people using technology to allow crops to grow.

landslide The rapid movement of soil and rock material down a slope.

latitude A region's distance from the equator, measured in degrees north or south.

levée An embankment, generally constructed close to the banks of a river, stream or lake, intended to protect the surrounding land from flooding.

meandering The looping and winding of a river within its floodplain.

mineral A chemical substance in the Earth's crust.

monsoon A seasonal shift in winds over large areas of land, caused by a dramatic changes in temperature.

permeable Able to absorb water easily.

precipitation The various forms of water – rain, snow, sleet and hail – that fall to the Earth's surface.

rain-shadow area An area on the sheltered side of a mountain range that receives low levels of rainfall.

rapids Fast-flowing parts of a river.

reservoir An artificial lake, often contained by a dam, used to generate a water supply or control the amount of water in a river to help prevent flood or drought.

runoff The part of rainfall that reaches streams or rivers; the remainder either evaporates into the atmosphere or seeps below ground.

saturated A condition of a material, such as soil, when it cannot absorb any more water.

sediment The solid that settles at the bottom of a liquid.

silt Very fine soil particles deposited by rivers.

soil erosion The process by which loose soil is washed or blown away.

soluble Capable of being dissolved.

source The place where a stream or river begins to flow.

spring tide A tide that is higher than normal, which occurs when the Sun and the Moon are aligned and are both exerting a strong gravitational force on the Earth's water.

stomata The 'pores' found on the underside of leaves on plants and trees, through which water is transpired.

storm surge An abnormal rise in sea level, usually caused by an area of low pressure over a body of water, and responsible for coastal flooding.

subsidence The sinking of land.

terracing The process of cutting steep steps in the side of a slope or hill to prevent fertile topsoil being washed away.

tide A regular movement of sea water towards and away from the land; caused by the gravity exerted by the Sun and Moon on the Earth.

topsoil The fertile upper layer of soil, in which plants and crops grow best.

transpiration The process by which plants release water vapour into the atmosphere through openings in their leaves.

tributary A stream or other body of water that contributes its water to another body of water.

tsunami A giant ocean wave – often called a tidal wave – caused by an undersea earthquake, volcanic eruption or landslide.

volcano A crack in the Earth's crust through which molten rock and lava erupts.

water cycle The constant and repeated movement of water between the air, land and sea.

water table The upper level of saturated soil or rock.

Further Information

Books

Wild Weather: Drought by Catherine Chambers: Heinemann, 2008

Famine and Drought by J. Walker: Franklin Watts, 2002

Floods by Catherine Chambers: Disasters in Nature, Heinemann, 2000

Floods by Emma Durham and Mark Maslin: Restless Planet, Wayland, 2000

Hurricane by Jack Challoner: Eyewitness Guides, Dorling Kindersley, 2004

Living with the Weather: Heat and Drought by Lionel Bender: Wayland, 1998

Raging Floods by Louise and Richard Spilsbury: Heinemann Library, 2004

The Kingfisher Geography Encyclopaedia by Clive Gifford: Kingfisher Publications, 2003

Web sites

http://www.dartmouth.edu/~floods/
The home page of the Dartmouth Flood Observatory, which contains analyses of flood events around the world using satellite images which feature on the web site.

http://www.drought.gov/
The National Integrated Drought Information System's (NIDIS) drought information centre, carrying information on drought and climate conditions.

http://www.redcross.org/
This site has a section on preparing for emergencies, including flooding and drought.

http://www.unwater.org/worldwaterday/
Website of the UN World Water Day.

http://www.unicef.org/drought/
Updated accounts of drought disasters facing many countries around the world.

http://www.usgs.gov/
The home page of the US Geological Survey, with vast amounts of resources and news stories about the geography and geology of the United States.

Index

Aceh, Indonesia 25
Africa 27, 32, 35
agriculture 6, 7, 14, 31, 36, 37
air 9, 10, 23, 28
air pollution 15
air pressure 9, 12, 22, 23, 42
Aleutian Islands 25
all-India drought 27
alluvial plains 17
animals 26, 33
Antarctic 11
anticyclones 12
aquifers 10, 42
Asia 12, 17, 28, 35
Asian tsunami 25
Aswan High Dam, Egypt 38, 39
atmosphere 8, 9, 10, 11, 12, 14, 15, 28, 29, 42
Australia 6, 12, 13, 14, 28, 31, 33
Awa, Japan 25
bacteria 6
Badger, Canada 19
Bangladesh 15, 23, 37
Bay of Fundy, Canada 24
bays 24
beaches 25
Big Thompson river valley flood 18, 20
blocking high 29, 30, 42
blue whales 6
bore holes 36
Buffalo Creek, USA 21
Cairo, Egypt 17
California, USA 13, 30
Cambodia 37
Canada 19, 29, 33
car parks 21
carbon dioxide 15
Central America 13, 28
chemicals 35
Chibuto, Mozambique 22
China 16, 19, 38
cholera 35
circulation cells 12
cities 36, 37
civil war 27
civilisations 17
clay 10

climate 8, 10, 12, 13, 14, 26, 29, 33, 34, 42
clouds 9, 12, 23, 28, 29, 31
coal-mining 21
coasts 12, 15, 21, 22, 25, 37
  coastal flooding 12, 22, 37
Colorado, USA 20
communications 7, 41
concrete 21
contamination 7, 42
continental drought regions 31, 42
crops 7, 16, 17, 31, 32, 34, 38
cyclones 12
dams 18, 20, 21, 38, 39, 40
deaths 7, 19, 20, 21, 25, 26, 32
deforestation 14, 15, 20, 33, 34, 42
Delta Plan, Netherlands 39
deltas 15, 17, 42
deposition 16, 17
depressions 12
desalination 37, 42
desertification 33, 42
deserts 26, 28, 34
disaster relief 32
disease 7, 23, 25, 27, 35, 38
domestic sewage 36
drainage basins 18, 42
droughts 6, 7, 8, 13, 14, 15, 26, 27, 29, 32, 34, 35, 36, 41, 42
  predicting 41
Dust Bowl 35
Earth 6, 9, 10, 11, 12, 24, 41
earthquakes 24, 25, 42
Ecuador 10
El Niño 13, 14, 29, 41, 42
energy 8, 10, 11, 15, 21, 25
England 12
equator 10, 11, 12, 42
erosion 16, 25, 32, 38, 42
Ethiopia 27, 28, 32, 35
Europe 12, 27, 30
evaporation 8, 15, 28, 33, 34, 42
evapotranspiration 29, 42
Exploits River, Canada 19
famine 7, 27, 31, 42

farming 34, 38
fertile 7, 37, 42
fertilisers 36, 38
fires 16, 31
fishing 37
flash floods 13, 20, 42
flood barriers 39
floodplains 16, 17, 42
floods 6, 7, 8, 12, 13, 14, 15, 16, 17, 18, 19, 21, 24, 32, 34, 41, 42
  benefits of 7, 37
  bonna 38
  borsha 38
  cloudburst 20, 42
  coastal 12, 22, 37
  control 38, 39
  measuring 18
  predicting 40
  river 18
Florida, USA 23
food 17, 23, 27, 31, 32
  aid 32
  distribution 27
  supplies 29
fossil fuels 15, 42
freezing 10, 18
freshwater 6, 26, 35, 36, 37
Ganges, India 17, 23, 38
gas 6
Gift of the Nile 17
global heat balance 12
global warming 14, 15, 22, 29, 31, 42
Gobi Desert, Mongolia 31
gravity 24
Great Dividing Range, Australia 30
greenhouse effect 14, 15, 42
greenhouse gases 14, 15, 43
ground 8, 10, 12, 20, 32, 36
groundwater 10, 26, 43
Gulf of Mexico 12, 16
Gulf Stream 12
hail 9
heat 8, 12, 15, 28, 29
Hilo, USA 25
Himalayas 37
homelessness 23, 32, 38
Huang He, China 17, 19
human activity 20, 21, 33

human life 17
humidity 9, 29, 43
hurricanes 12, 22, 23, 41, 43
  Hurricane Frances 23
hydroelectric power plants 21
Ice 6, 17, 18
  crystals 9
  ice jams 19, 20, 43
India 26, 37
Indian Ocean 25
Indonesia 13, 25, 38
Indus, India 17
industry 15, 21, 36
infiltration 10, 20, 32, 43
infrastructures 7, 42
inland 8, 12, 25, 31
Intergovernmental Panel on Climate Change 15
irrigation 39, 43
Kabul 28
Karaktoa, Indonesia 25
Kenya 32
lakes 6, 7, 8, 20, 26
land mining 33
landslides 7, 21, 24, 43
latitude 10, 12, 43
leaves 9, 34
levées 38, 43
life on Earth 6
liquid 6, 8
livestock 31, 33
Longarone, Italy 21
magnitude 18
maize 29
meandering 16, 43
meltwater 18
methane 15
Middle East 35, 37
Middle of the Earth monument, Ecuador 10
migration 34
Mississippi River, USA 16, 40
moisture 9, 29, 31
monsoons 17, 26, 43
Moon 24
Morocco 33
motor vehicles 15
mountains 20, 30
mudslides 7

mulching 34
Murray-Darling Basin,
    Australia 14
natural disasters 16, 31
natural hazards 6, 7
Netherlands 12, 39, 40
Nicaragua 25
Nile, Egypt 17, 38, 39
nitrates 37
nitrous oxide 15
nomadic peoples 34
North America 29
North Dakota, USA 26
North Sea 12
Northern Hemisphere 33
ocean currents 12, 13, 29
ocean storms 22
oceans 8, 10, 12, 14, 25, 31
organisms 6
overgrazing 33, 34
Palmer Drought Severity
    Index 27
pavements 21
permeability 18, 43
phosphates 37
plants 7, 8, 9, 10, 20, 26, 32,
    33, 35
polar ice caps 19
polar regions 11, 12
pollution 36
pools 10
populations 22, 35, 37, 41
porosity 18
poverty 31
precipitation 9, 31, 43
Pribilof Islands, USA 24
puddles 10
rain 6, 7, 9, 10, 12, 13, 17,
    18, 20, 21, 26, 27, 28, 29,
    30, 31, 32, 33, 34, 40
    rainfall average 26
rain-shadow areas 30, 43
rain-shadow effect 30
reforestation 34, 39
refugee camps 32
rescue workers 25
reservoirs 21, 38, 39, 43
rice 16
Richter scale 25
rivers 6, 7, 8, 10, 16, 17, 20,
    33, 38
    banks 17, 18, 40
    channels 18
    floods 18

mature 16
    young 16
roads 21, 25
rock 21
Rocky Mountains, USA 30
roots 8, 20, 33
Sahara Desert, Africa 27,
    28, 33
Sahel, Africa 33
saltwater 37
sand 10, 25
sanitation 35
saturation 18, 43
saturation zone 10
scientists 12, 14, 40
sea levels 12, 15, 22, 24
seas 12, 14, 16, 39
    inland seas 6
seawater 6, 24
sediments 16, 17, 20, 33, 37,
    38, 43
settlements 7, 21, 25
sewage systems 7, 35
silt 19, 43
sleet 9, 10
snow 9, 10, 12, 17, 18
snowmelt 19, 20
soil 7, 8, 16, 18, 20, 29, 30,
    32, 34, 38
    composition of 10
    management 34
soil erosion 35, 43
Somalia 32
sorghum 34, 35
South America 13
South East Asia 13, 34
standpipes 26
stomata 9, 43
stone 21
storm surges 12, 18, 22, 39,
    43
storms 14, 18, 23
storm-surge barriers 39, 40
streams 7, 10, 18
Sudan 32
sulphur dioxide 33
Sun 8, 10, 11, 12, 15, 23, 24
supplies 23
surface runoff 10, 18, 20, 21,
    38, 43
technology 40, 41
temperature 9, 10, 12,
    27, 29
    temperature records 14

Tennessee Valley Authority
    38
terracing 16, 38, 39, 43
Texas, USA 29
Thailand 32
Thames, UK 24, 39
thunderstorms 20
tides 24, 43
    spring tides 24, 43
    tidal range 24
topsoil 33, 35, 43
towns 36, 37
transpiration 8, 9, 10, 28,
    34, 43
transport systems 7, 41
trees 14, 15, 20, 33
tributaries 18, 43
tropics 23
tsunamis 22, 24, 25, 43
typhoons 12, 23
UK 21, 26
underground channels 18
United Nations 33
United States 13, 16, 26, 27,
    28, 31, 35, 40
uplands 16
urbanisation 21
US Environmental
    Protection Agency 15
Vaiont Dam, Italy 21
vegetation 25, 33, 34
vehicles 20
Venice, Italy 22
villages 7, 36
volcanic eruptions 24, 25
volcanoes 25, 43
water 6, 8, 9, 10, 12, 18, 21,
    26, 27, 29, 30, 32, 35, 36,
    37, 38
    conservation 36
    distribution 6, 35, 36
    droplets 9
    levels 34
    movement 8, 10
    proportions 14
    rationing 36
    resources 36
    supplies 7, 31
    systems 32
water cycle 8, 15, 19, 28, 43
water table 10, 43
water tankers 26
water vapour 6, 8, 9, 28, 31
waves 21, 24

weather 12, 15, 29
    conditions 8
    forecasting 41
    patterns 10, 14
wells 36
windbreaks 34
winds 9, 10, 12, 29, 30
    speeds 23
winter 12, 18
World Health Organization
    35
World Meteorological
    Organisation 41
Yangtze, China 19
Yellowstone Park, USA 29

Acknowledgements

About the author

Clive Gifford is the author of more than 60 books, including *The Kingfisher Geography Encyclopedia* and *Living Worlds* – which explains Earth's natural cycles and the interactions between the millions of lifeforms that have helped shape and create the world in which we live – for which he received the Smithsonian Museum's Notable Books for Children award. His book *Refugees*, part of the World Issues series, was also nominated for the 2003 British Book Awards. He travels widely and has given hundreds of lectures for children, both in the UK and abroad, on geographical issues and processes.

About the consultant

Simon Ross is Head of Geography at Queen's College in Taunton, Somerset. He has published extensively on all aspects of physical geography, from introductory level to upper secondary. His books include *Natural Hazards*, *Introducing Physical Geography and Map Reading*, and several books in the series Geography 21. He has worked as editor on many series, including Longman Co-Ordinated Geography and Longman Exploring Geography. He has also acted as consultant on television programmes for the BBC, and for the QCA on Geography Key Stage 3 resources. He regularly lectures and contributes articles to encyclopedias and journals.

Picture Credits

Cover: (t) Grunewald Olivier/OSF **(bl)** Ted Mead/OSF **(br)** Mauro Fermariello/Science Photo Library **6(t)** NASA/OSF **6(b)** Paul Nevin/OSF **7** Jean-Leo Dugast/Still Pictures **9(t)** Stephen J. Krasemann/Science Photo Library **9(b)** VVG/ Science Photo Library **10(b)** © Pablo Corral V/Corbis **11(b)** Emmanuel Jeanjean/ Still Pictures **12** 2002 Orbital Imaging Corporation/Science Photo Library **13(l)** Grunewald Olivier/ OSF **14(l)** © Gallo Images/Corbis **14(r)** Ted Mead/OSF **15(b)** C. Allen Morgan/Still Pictures **16** C.K.Au/UNEP/ Still Pictures **17(b)** Earth Satellite Corporation/Science Photo Library **19(t)** UNEP/Still Pictures **19(b)** Argus/ Still Pictures **20** Jim Reed/Science Photo Library **21(t)** Eco **21(b)** © Bettman/Corbis **22(t)** Mauro Fermariello/Science Photo Library **22(b)** Per-Anders Petersson/UNEP/Still Pictures **23(t)** © Jayanta Shaw/ Reuters/Corbis **23(b)** © Marc Serota/Reuters/Corbis **24(t)** © Tim Thompson/Corbis **25(t)** © Stringer/Malaysia/Reuters/Corbis **25(b)** © Keith Dannemiller/Corbis **26(t)** © Royalty-free/Corbis **27** David McNew/Still Pictures **28(t)** © Reuters/Corbis **28(b)** Frans Lemmens/Still Pictures **29** Mike Boyatt/ Agstock/ Science Photo Library **30(t)** Kevin Lane/UNEP/Still Pictures **31** Nigel Dickinson/Still Pictures **32(t)** Mark Edwards/Still Pictures **32(b)** Kittprempool-UNEP/Still Pictures **33(t)** Eco **33(b)** Voltchev/UNEP/Still Pictures **34** © Gary Braasch/ Corbis **35(t)** © Bettmann/Corbis **35(b)** Pieternella Pieterse/Still Pictures **37(t)** Bojan Brecelj/Still Pictures **37(b)** © Kevin R. Morris/Corbis **38** Friedrich Stark/Still Pictures **39(t)** Jorgen Schytte/Still Pictures **40(t)** © Cees Van Leeuwen; Cordaly Photo Library Ltd/ Corbis **40(b)** © Andrew Holbrooke/Corbis **41** © Bettmann/Corbis